THE HOW, WHAT & WHY
OF MAMMALS

GARETH COLEMAN

Acknowledgements

Photos: Andy Rouse, page 9 top. Stuart MacFarlane, page 9 bottom. Professor P M Motta, G Macchiarelli, S A Nottola/Science Photo Library, page 17. Heather Angel, page 21. Andrew J Purcell/Bruce Coleman Ltd, page 26. Jane Burton/Bruce Coleman Ltd, page 29.

Illustrations: John Butler/Ian Fleming Associates, page 4. Ed Stuart, pages 5, 15, 16, 20, 22, 23, 24 top. Mike Atkinson/Garden Studio, pages 6 top, 7 top, 8, 12-13, 14. Doreen McGuinness/Garden Studio, contents top right, bottom right, pages 6-7 bottom, 10 top, 27, 30, bottom left. Miranda Gray/Maggie Mundy, contents top left, pages 10 bottom, 11 top, 24 bottom, 25, 28, 29. Steve Weston/Linden Artists, pages 18-19.

Heinemann Educational Publishers
Halley Court, Jordan Hill, Oxford OX2 8EJ
a division of Reed Educational and Professional Publishing Limited
www.heinemann.co.uk

Heinemann is a registered trademark of Reed Educational and Professional Publishing Limited

First published 2000
Original edition © Reed Educational and Professional Publishing, 1999
Literacy Satellites edition © Reed Educational and Professional Publishing Limited, 2000
Additional writing for Satellites edition by Wendy Cobb

04 03 02 01 00
10 9 8 7 6 5 4 3 2 1

ISBN 0 435 11961 3 *The How, What and Why of Mammals* single copy
ISBN 0 435 11965 6 *The How, What and Why of Mammals* 6 copy pack

All rights reserved. No part of this publication may be reproduced or transmitted in any form, or by any means, electronic or mechanical, including photocopy, recording or any information storage and retrieval system without permission in writing from the publishers.

Designed by Traffika Publishing Limited
Printed and bound in Scotland by Scotprint

Also available at Stage 3 Literacy World Satellites
ISBN 0 435 11960 5 *LW Satellites: Extracts from Zlata's Diary* single copy
ISBN 0 435 11964 8 *LW Satellites: Extracts from Zlata's Diary* 6 copy pack

ISBN 0 435 11962 1 *LW Satellites: Broomsticks and Balloons* single copy
ISBN 0 435 11966 4 *LW Satellites: Broomsticks and Balloons* 6 copy pack

ISBN 0 435 11963 X *LW Satellites: How to Persuade People* single copy
ISBN 0 435 11967 2 *LW Satellites: How to Persuade People* 6 copy pack

ISBN 0 435 11969 9 *LW Satellites: Teachers' Guide Stage 3*
ISBN 0 435 11968 0 *LW Satellites: Guided Reading Cards Stage 3*

Contents

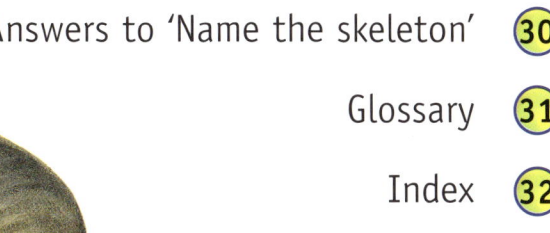

What are mammals? — 4
What is a skeleton? — 6
What are muscles? — 8
How do mammals move? — 10
Why do mammals eat? — 12
Why do mammals breathe? — 14
What does the heart do? — 16
How does a mammal's brain work? — 18
How do mammals smell? — 20
How do mammals hear? — 22
How do mammals see? — 24
How do mammals use camouflage? — 26
How do mammals' babies grow? — 28

Answers to 'Name the skeleton' — 30
Glossary — 31
Index — 32

What are mammals?

Mammals are a group of animals. There are 4000 different kinds of mammals. The biggest whale in the world is a mammal. So is the smallest mouse.

How are mammals the same?

All mammals have warm blood. We call them warm-blooded. Their body temperature stays the same even if it is very hot or very cold outside.

All mammals have hair. But it is not always like our hair. It can be fur, wool, whiskers, spines, prickles or horns! The hair keeps out the cold and keeps the mammal warm.

Baby mammals feed on their mother's milk. This is called suckling. Mammals look after their young for much longer than other animals.

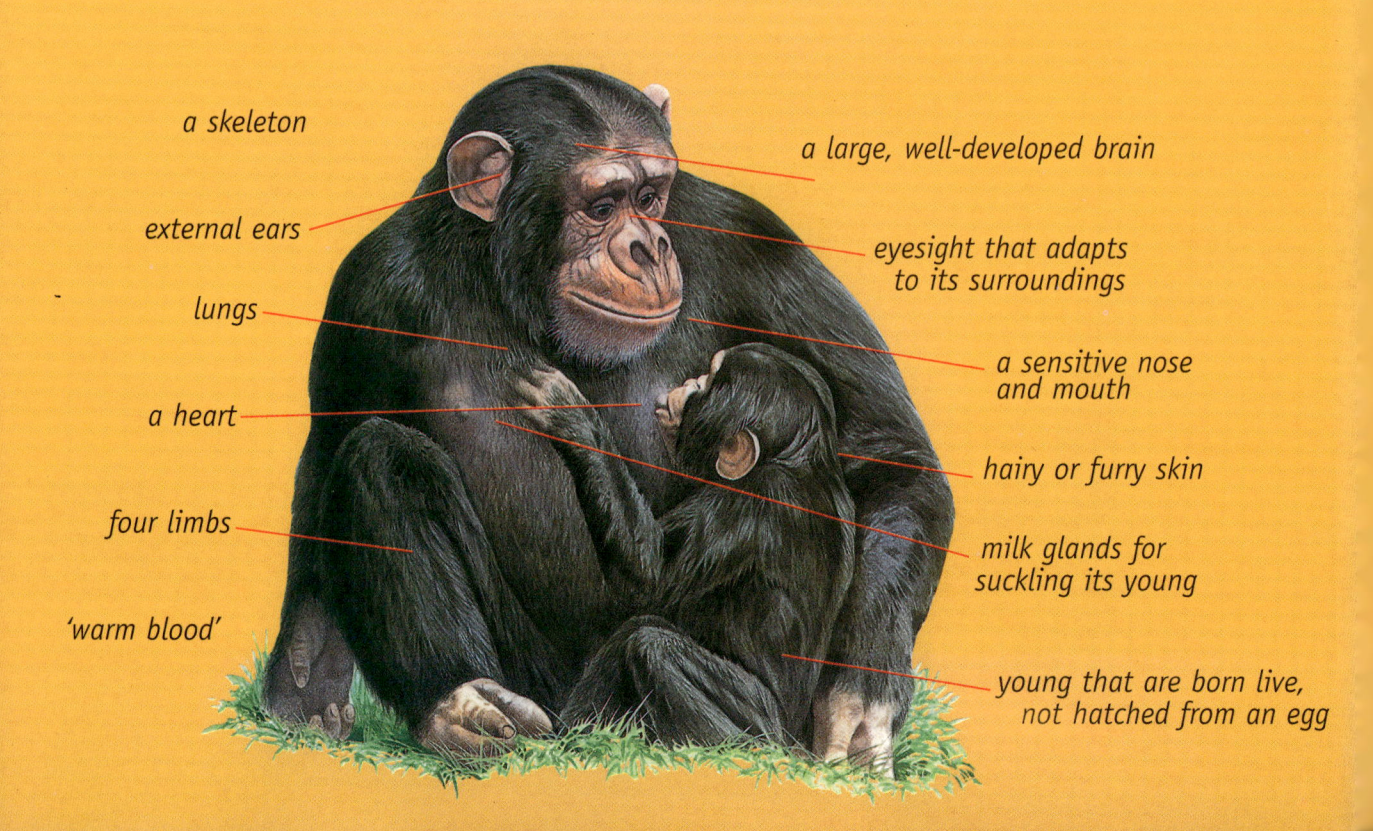

- a skeleton
- external ears
- lungs
- a heart
- four limbs
- 'warm blood'
- a large, well-developed brain
- eyesight that adapts to its surroundings
- a sensitive nose and mouth
- hairy or furry skin
- milk glands for suckling its young
- young that are born live, not hatched from an egg

How long have mammals been on Earth?

The evolution of life

Look at the time-line. Can you see that mammals are the latest animals to evolve on Earth? They appeared about 200 million years ago. The first mammals were probably tiny – about the size of mice. They probably lived on insects and dinosaur eggs. When the dinosaurs died out, the mammals evolved to take over as the most important group of animals.

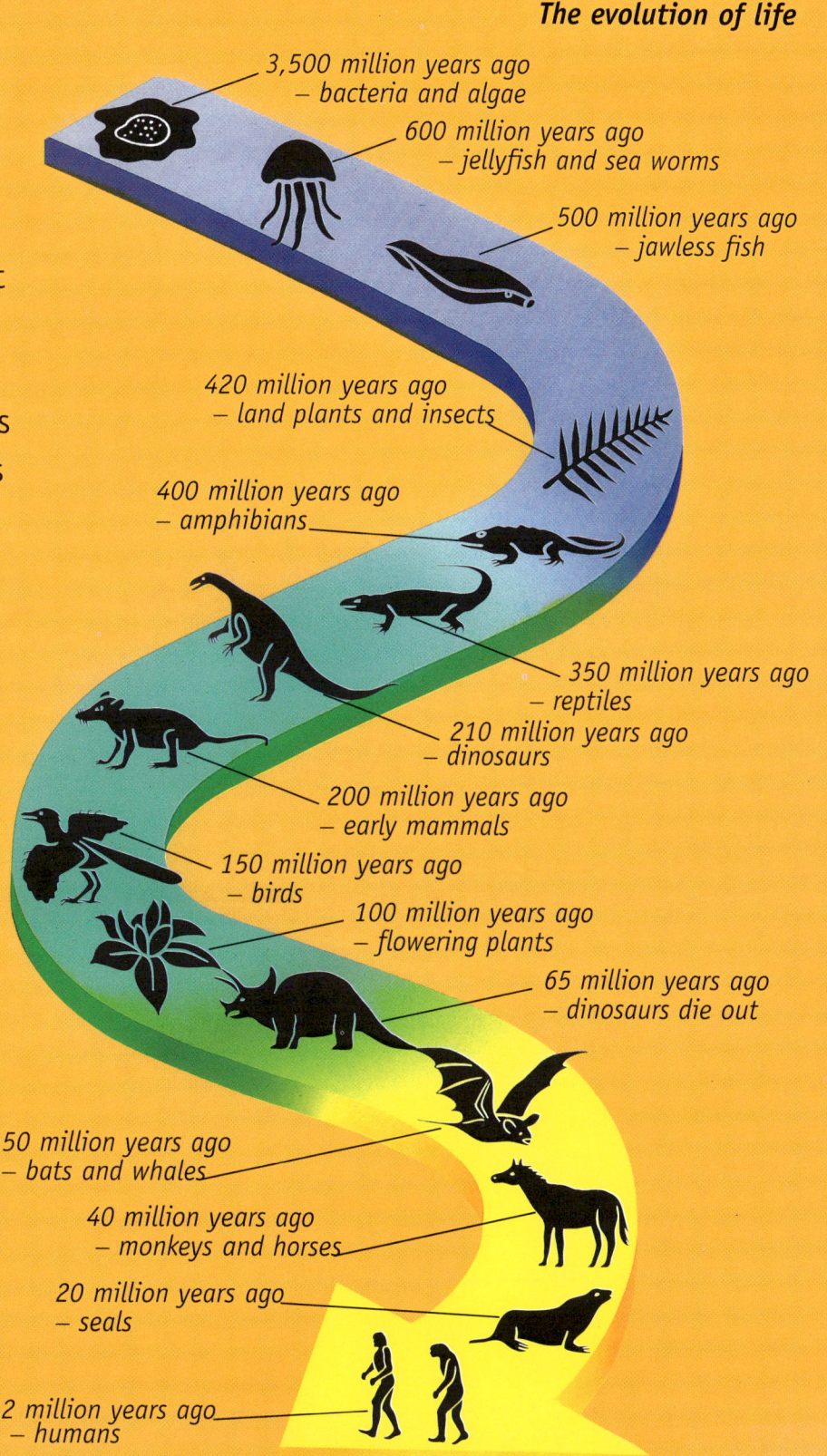

- 3,500 million years ago – bacteria and algae
- 600 million years ago – jellyfish and sea worms
- 500 million years ago – jawless fish
- 420 million years ago – land plants and insects
- 400 million years ago – amphibians
- 350 million years ago – reptiles
- 210 million years ago – dinosaurs
- 200 million years ago – early mammals
- 150 million years ago – birds
- 100 million years ago – flowering plants
- 65 million years ago – dinosaurs die out
- 50 million years ago – bats and whales
- 40 million years ago – monkeys and horses
- 20 million years ago – seals
- 2 million years ago – humans

What is a skeleton?

A skeleton is made up of many bones. All mammals have a skeleton inside their body. It is made up of a skull, a backbone, a rib cage, hip bones, limbs.

Because they have a skeleton, mammals can stand up and move about.

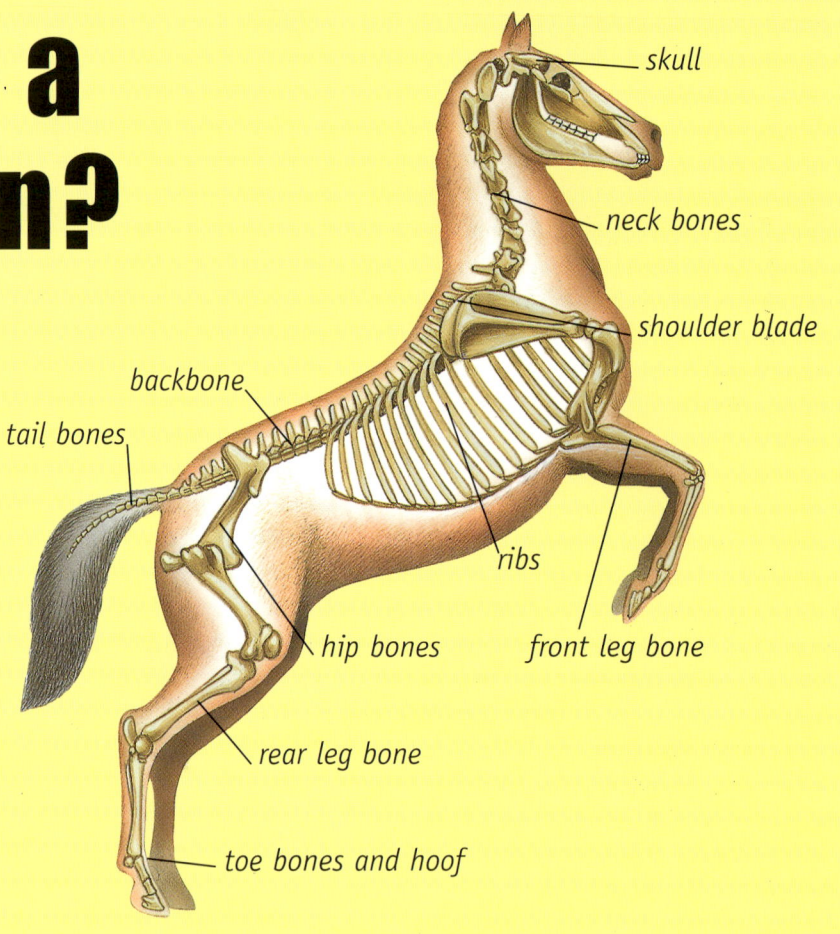

skull
neck bones
shoulder blade
backbone
tail bones
ribs
front leg bone
hip bones
rear leg bone
toe bones and hoof

Name the skeleton

Different mammals have different kinds of skeleton. Their skeletons have evolved to meet their needs. A horse has long, thin leg bones so that it can run fast. A giraffe has long neck bones so that it can reach the top of tall trees.

Can you work out which mammals have these skeletons?
(See page 30 for answers)

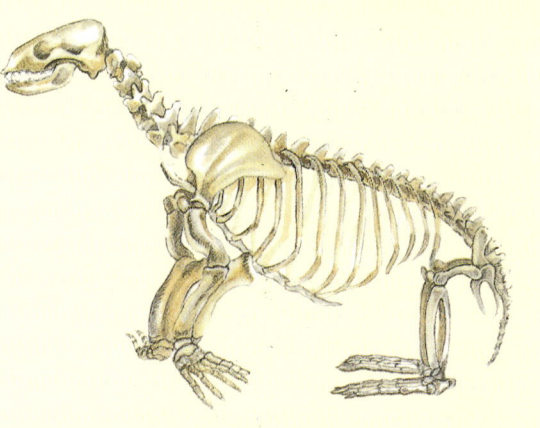

1. This mammal has big shoulders and strong front legs to help it swim in the sea.

How many bones do humans have?

An adult human has about 206 bones, but a newborn baby has more than 800. Its body can bend, making it easier to be born. As it grows, many of its bones join together.

Why are humans' legs much longer than their arms?

Humans are the only mammals who spend most of their time walking on two feet. So our leg bones are much stronger than our arms. As we walk or run, the bones in our feet and toes push against the ground, enabling us to move.

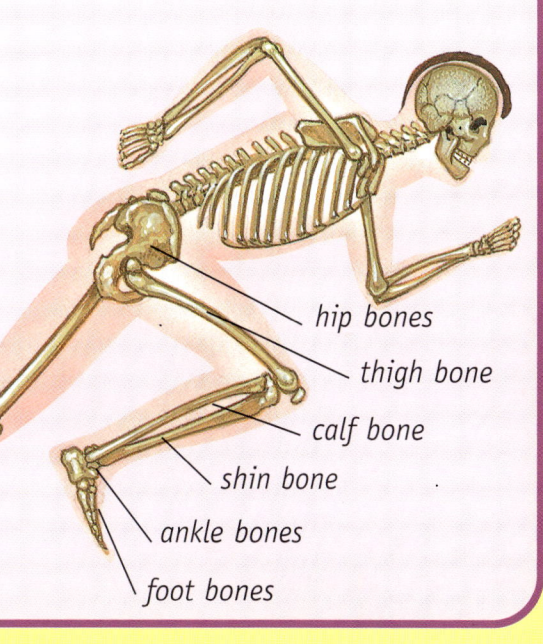

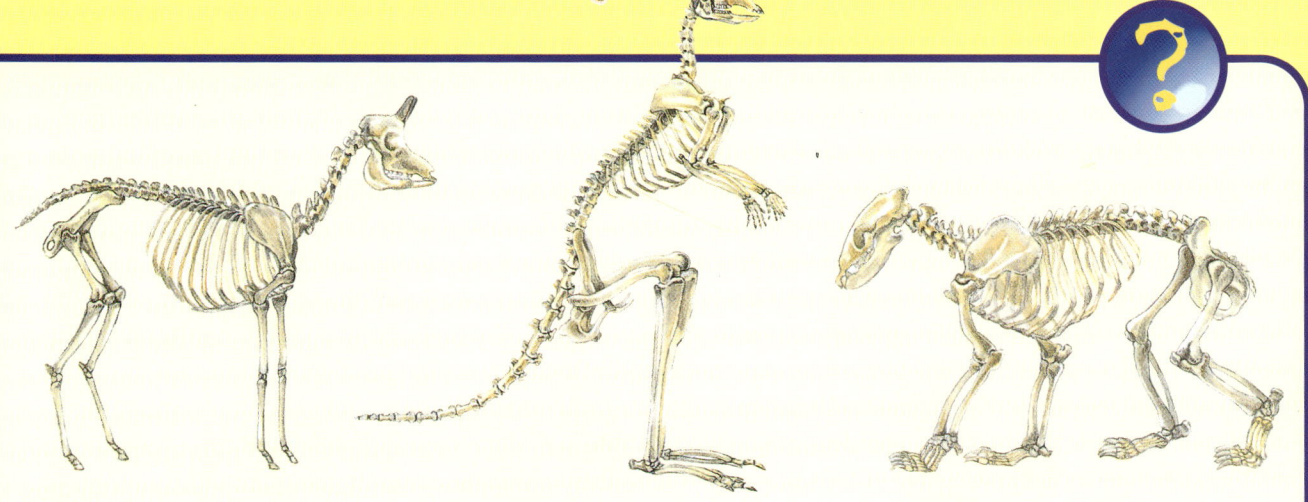

- hip bones
- thigh bone
- calf bone
- shin bone
- ankle bones
- foot bones

2. This mammal has long, slim legs. It can run very quickly to escape from predators.

3. The strong back legs of this mammal help it to leap away from danger. Its tail helps it to balance.

4. This mammal has four legs of the same size, so it is likely to walk slowly.

What are muscles?

Muscles pull bones to make the animal move. Each muscle is made of many fibres. The animal's brain tells the fibres when to get shorter (contract) or when to relax. Muscles are joined to bones and when the muscle contracts it moves the bones.

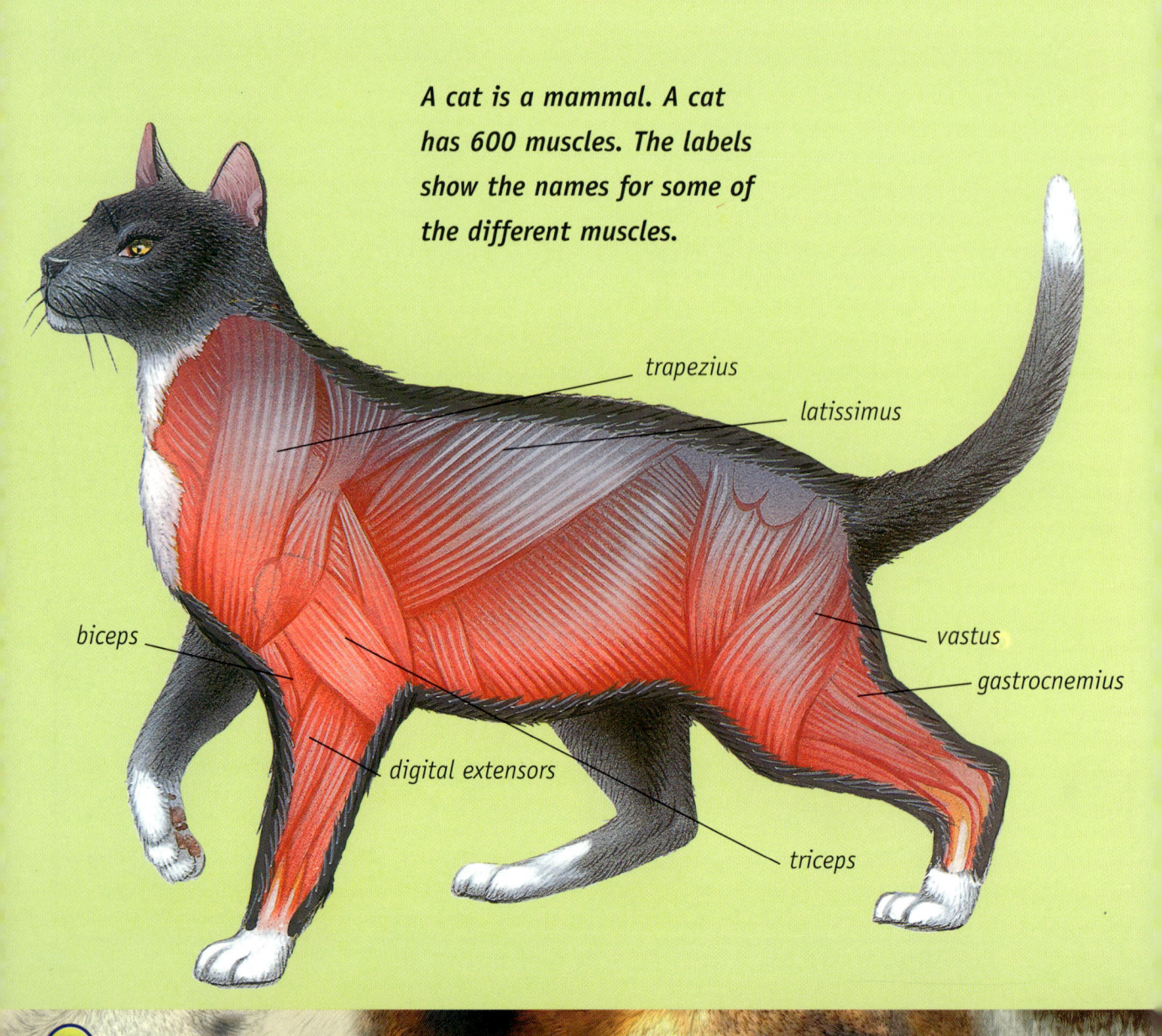

A cat is a mammal. A cat has 600 muscles. The labels show the names for some of the different muscles.

- trapezius
- latissimus
- vastus
- gastrocnemius
- biceps
- digital extensors
- triceps

Muscles in action

Muscles can pull but they can't push. So they work in pairs. First one pulls the bone and its partner relaxes. Then the partner pulls and the first one relaxes. The muscles take it in turn to contract and relax.

When a tiger runs, muscles contract to pull its legs forwards and backwards.

Why do weightlifters have big muscles?

The more a muscle is used, the bigger and stronger it gets. Weightlifters do exercises to make their muscles bigger. But a body can work well without very big muscles.

What is cramp?

Cramp is when a muscle suddenly contracts. Sometimes we strain it while exercising.
Or it can contract while we are asleep. Cramp can hurt a lot and can last several minutes before the muscle relaxes again.

How do mammals move?

Some mammals run, some fly and others swim. To help them move in these different ways, their skeletons and muscles have to be different.

Mammals on land

Most mammals live on land – walking, running, jumping or swinging. Cheetahs run fast to catch their prey. Kangaroos use their strong back legs to leap out of danger.

Orang-utans use their long arms and legs to swing through trees. Some monkeys have strong tails that they also use to hang from branches.

Mammals in water

Mammals that live in seas and rivers have bodies that help them move through the water. Dolphins and whales have muscles in their tails which they swish up and down to move forwards.

Otters have flaps of skin between their toes. As they swim, they spread their toes so their webbed feet push against the water.

Mammals in the air

Bats are the only mammals that can fly. Their arms and hands have evolved into wings. They have strong muscles in their chests so they can flap their wings and fly.

They can be tiny; only 14 centimetres from one wing tip to the other, or have a wingspan up to 2 metres!

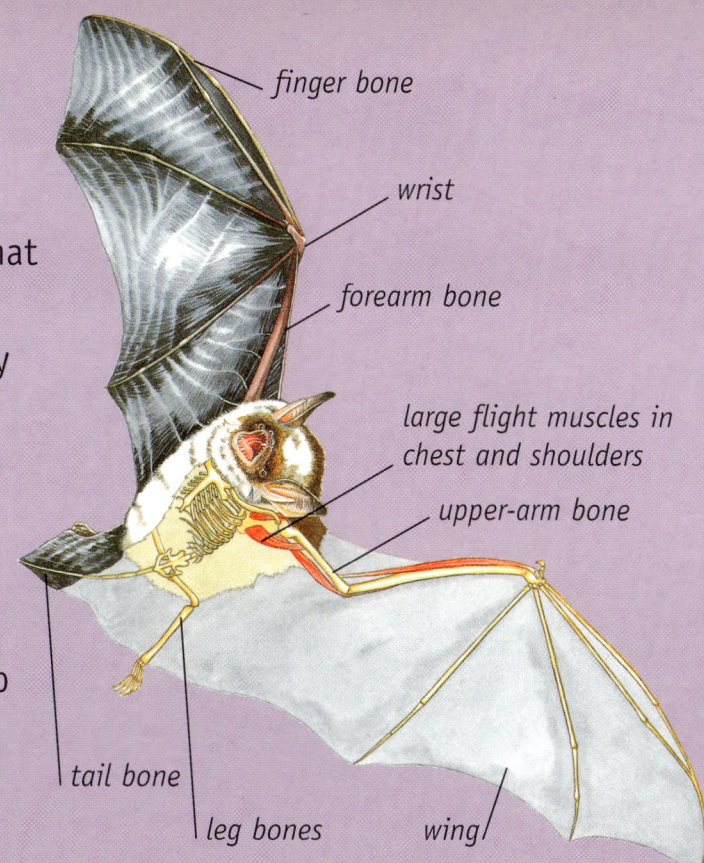

- finger bone
- wrist
- forearm bone
- large flight muscles in chest and shoulders
- upper-arm bone
- tail bone
- leg bones
- wing

How fast can a human run compared to other mammals?

Most mammals can run faster than a world champion. Animals need to run fast to catch their prey or run away from their predators.

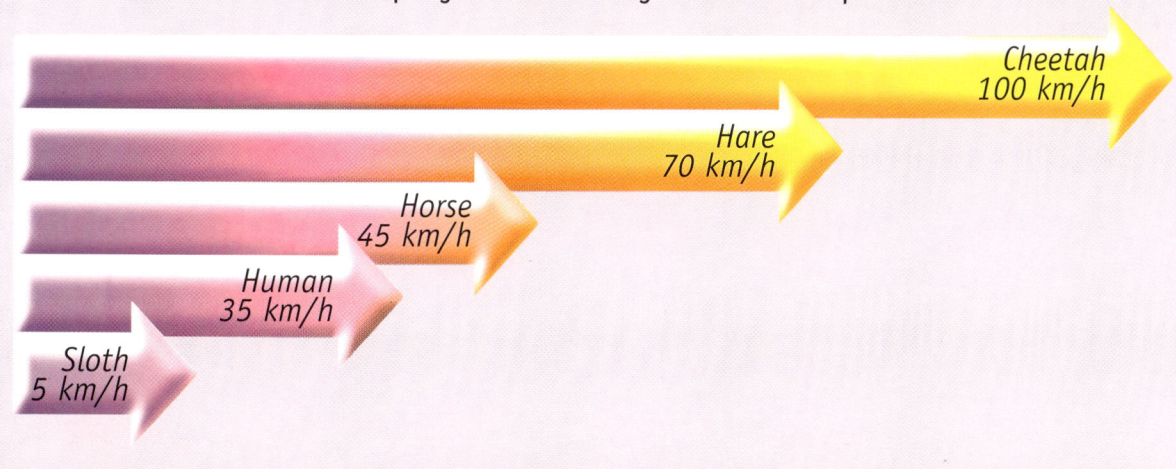

- Cheetah 100 km/h
- Hare 70 km/h
- Horse 45 km/h
- Human 35 km/h
- Sloth 5 km/h

The average running speed of different mammals

Why do mammals eat?

Mammals need food to grow, to stay healthy and to move. And they need to keep their bodies at the correct temperature.

From mouth to stomach

Mammals chew up their food into small pieces. It mixes with a juice called saliva.

Then they swallow it and the food goes down the gullet into the stomach. There it is mixed up with more juices until it turns into a thick liquid.

The intestines

Next, the food moves into the intestines. More juices mix with the food and break it down into all the nutrients that the body needs.

Then the nutrients are taken around the body by the blood. Some are stored by the body as fat. When there is not much food around, the animal can live off its fat. Waste food comes out of the end of the intestines.

salivary glands which produce saliva

teeth

tongue

gullet

Do humans need to eat meat?

Mammals eat different kinds of food. Some, like lions and tigers, eat meat. Their bodies can digest meat and get all the nutrients they need. They are called carnivores.

Others, like cows and elephants, eat plants. Their bodies have evolved to get all their nutrients from plant food. They are called herbivores.

Some animals, like dogs and humans, can eat meat and plants. They can digest both kinds of food. They are called omnivores.

Some people do not like to eat other animals so they never eat meat. They are called vegetarians. As long as they eat lots of different plants they can get all the nutrients they need.

small intestine

stomach

large intestine

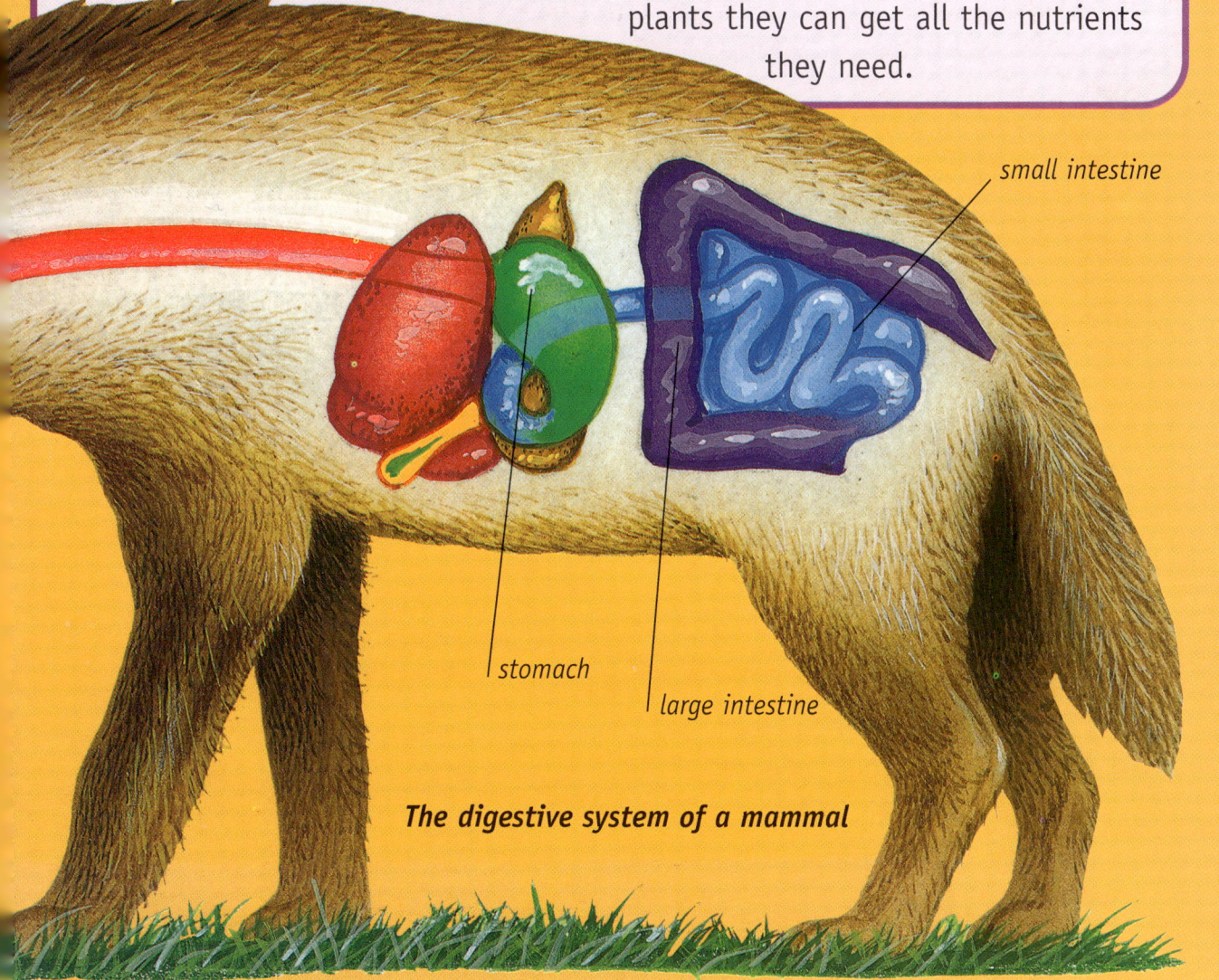

The digestive system of a mammal

Why do mammals breathe?

Mammals must have oxygen so their bodies can turn food into energy. They need energy to grow, move and keep warm. Mammals get oxygen into their bodies by breathing. All mammals have to breathe air, even whales and seals. They have to come above water for air.

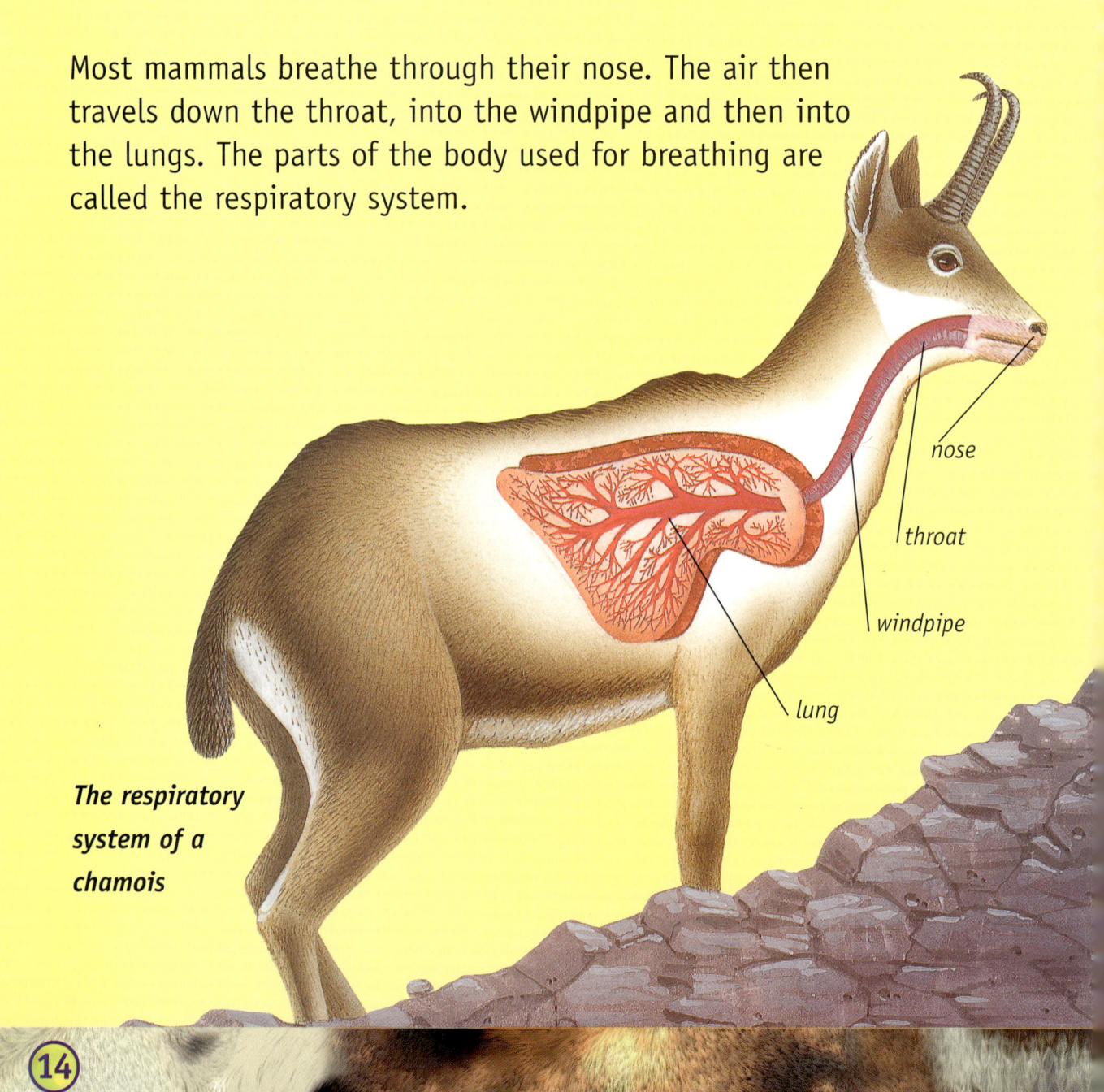

Most mammals breathe through their nose. The air then travels down the throat, into the windpipe and then into the lungs. The parts of the body used for breathing are called the respiratory system.

nose

throat

windpipe

lung

The respiratory system of a chamois

How does the respiratory system work?

Every mammal has two lungs in its chest. The end of the windpipe divides into two branches, each to one lung. The two branches divide again and again until they are very thin. At the end of these thin branches are bunches of air bubbles called alveoli. Tiny blood vessels around the alveoli pick up fresh oxygen from the air which the mammal has breathed into its lungs. The blood now carries this fresh oxygen around the mammal's body.

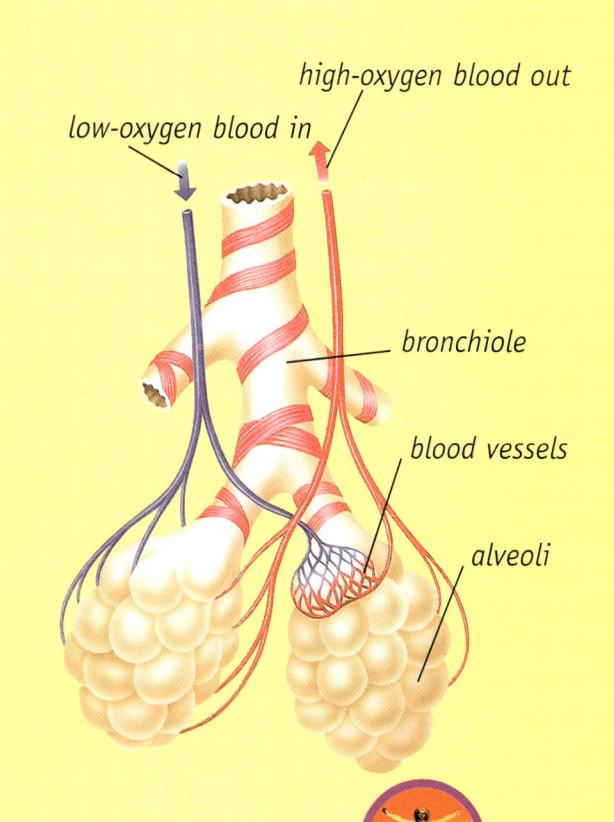

high-oxygen blood out
low-oxygen blood in
bronchiole
blood vessels
alveoli

What causes coughing?

Tiny specks of dust are sometimes breathed into the windpipe. They get stuck on the hairs inside it. So the brain tells the lungs to force some air up the windpipe, up the throat and out of the mouth. This makes a loud coughing noise and blows the dust out.

Why do I breathe faster when I exercise?

When we are resting we breathe in and out about 15 times a minute. But when we exercise, our muscles are working hard. Our muscles need extra oxygen to work well. So we have to breathe faster in order to get this extra oxygen to our muscles.

What does the heart do?

The heart is divided into two parts that do two different jobs. One part pumps blood to the lungs to pick up fresh supplies of oxygen. The other part pumps this high-oxygen blood around the rest of the body.

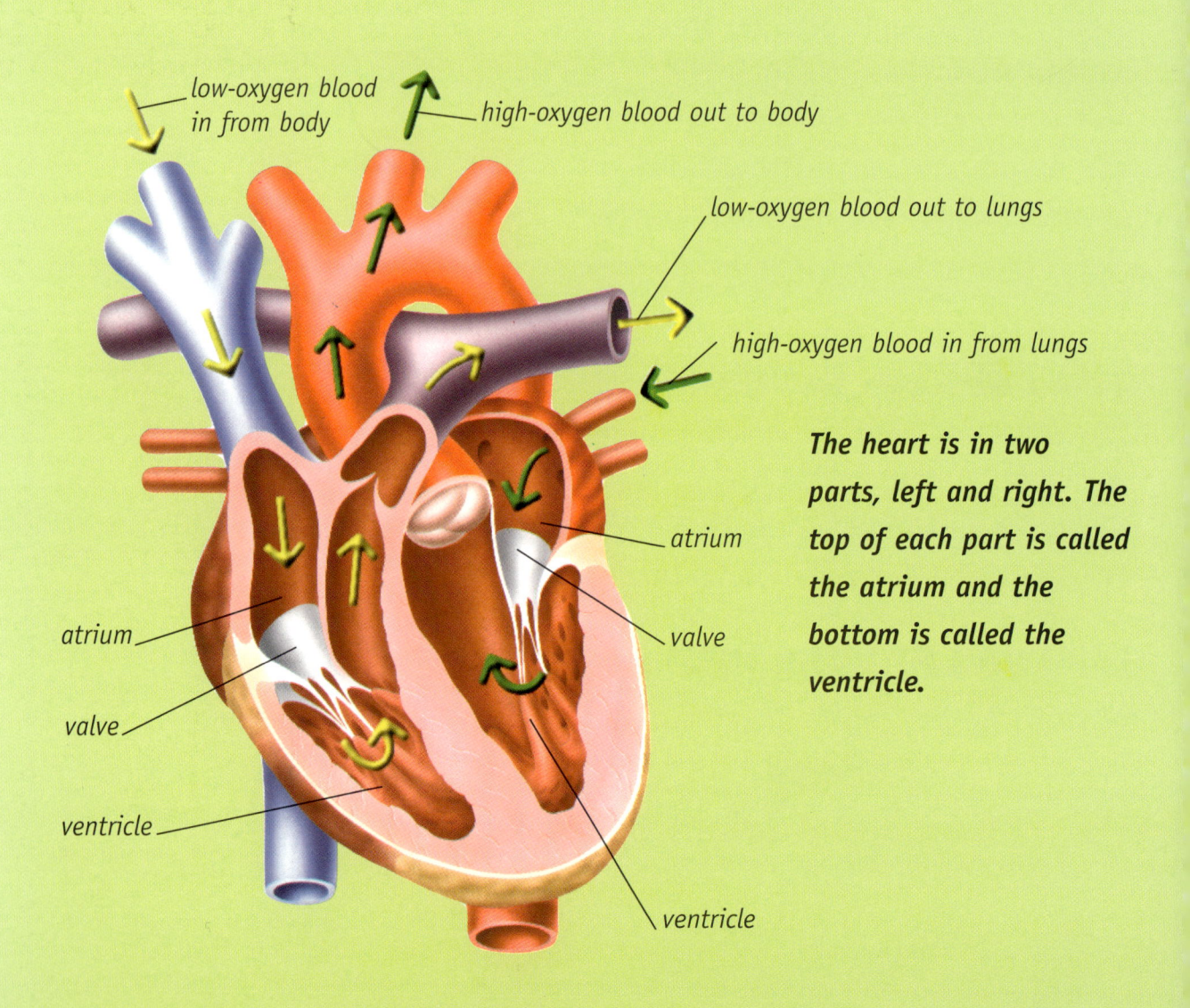

low-oxygen blood in from body

high-oxygen blood out to body

low-oxygen blood out to lungs

high-oxygen blood in from lungs

atrium

valve

ventricle

atrium

valve

ventricle

The heart is in two parts, left and right. The top of each part is called the atrium and the bottom is called the ventricle.

Warm blood

All mammals are warm-blooded. This means that the body of a mammal is always the same temperature. How does it manage to do this? If the animal gets too hot, more blood moves to the surface of the body and heat escapes through the skin. If the animal gets too cold, less blood goes to the surface so that all the heat is kept in the body.

Why do I bleed?

Human blood is made up of liquid, called plasma, and solid pieces, called blood cells and platelets. When the skin is cut, the plasma flows out, carrying the blood cells and platelets with it. The blood is pushed out by the pumping of the heart.

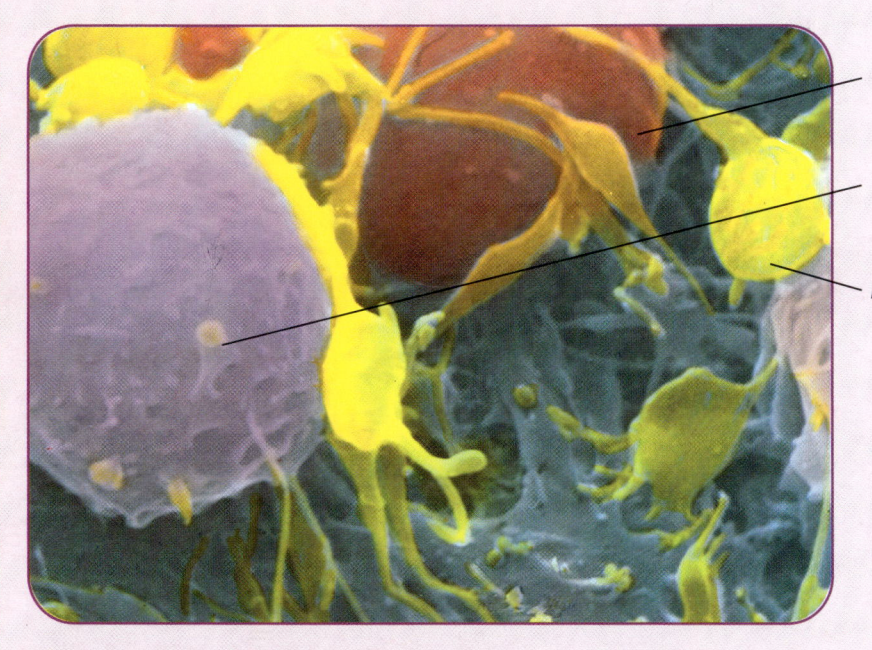

red blood cells

white blood cells

platelets

This photo, magnified 4,500 times, shows the cells and platelets in the blood.

How does the bleeding stop?

Soon after the bleeding starts, some of the platelets join together. They make a sort of tiny net. This net traps the blood cells so that the bleeding stops.

How does a mammal's brain work?

No one really understands how the brain works. But scientists have found that different parts of the brain do different jobs.

The **cerebrum** is the really big part of a mammal's brain. It takes in messages from the body and sends out messages to the muscles. And it does really important work, such as making up stories or doing sums in maths. This is the part which is working when we talk about 'using our brain'.

Why do I pull my hand away from something hot?

One of the ways we get messages to our brain is along our nerve cells. These send messages all around our body. Our eyes, ears, nose and tongue send messages about what we see, hear, smell or taste. And our skin sends messages about what we touch.

If we touch something hot, the nerves in the skin send a message to our brain at the speed of lightning. The brain sends a lightning-fast message back, telling the muscles to move away – fast! We call this a reflex action.

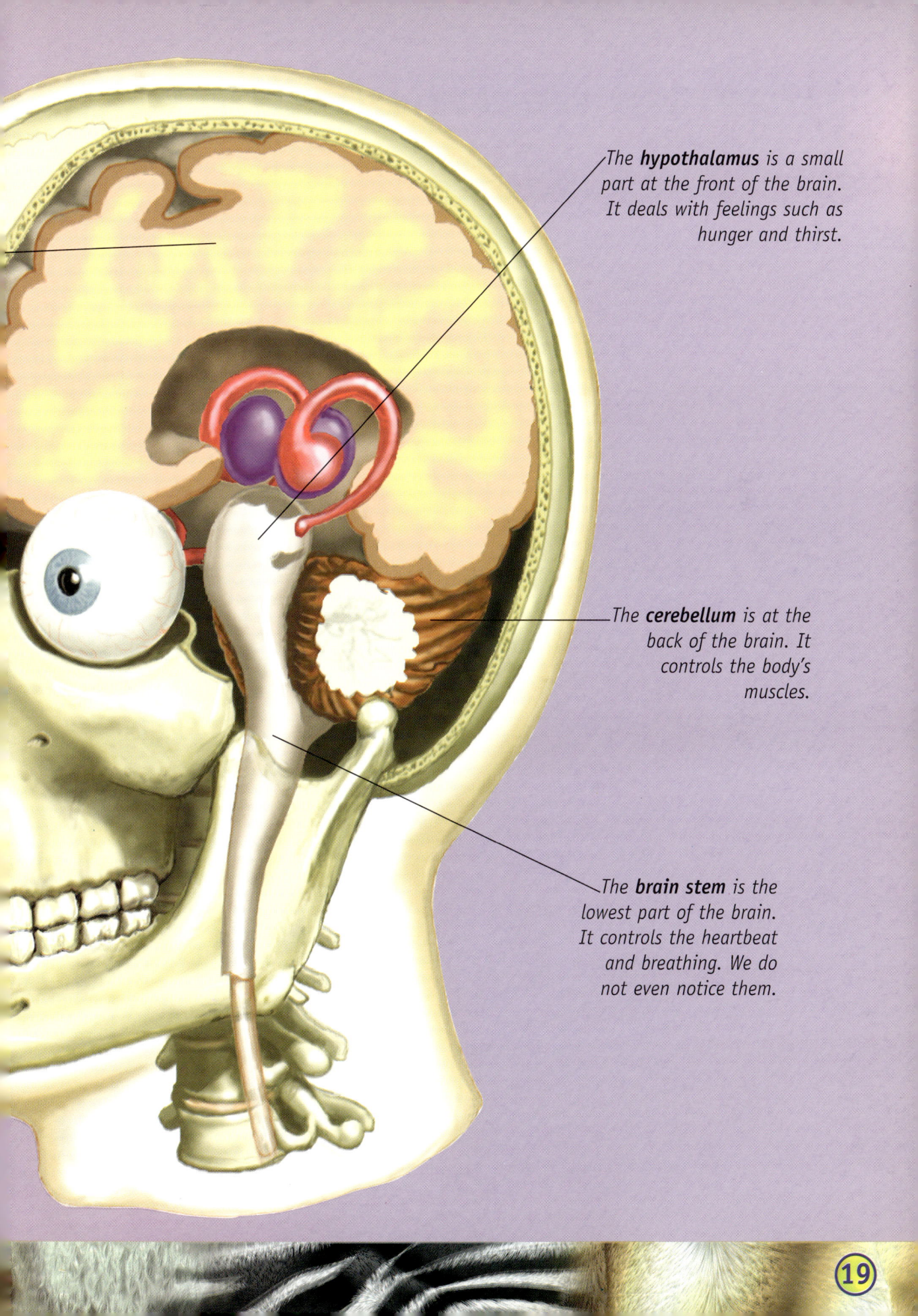

The **hypothalamus** is a small part at the front of the brain. It deals with feelings such as hunger and thirst.

The **cerebellum** is at the back of the brain. It controls the body's muscles.

The **brain stem** is the lowest part of the brain. It controls the heartbeat and breathing. We do not even notice them.

How do mammals smell?

Many mammals have a better sense of smell than humans and they use it to find food and escape from danger. The part of the body that we use is called the olfactory organ.

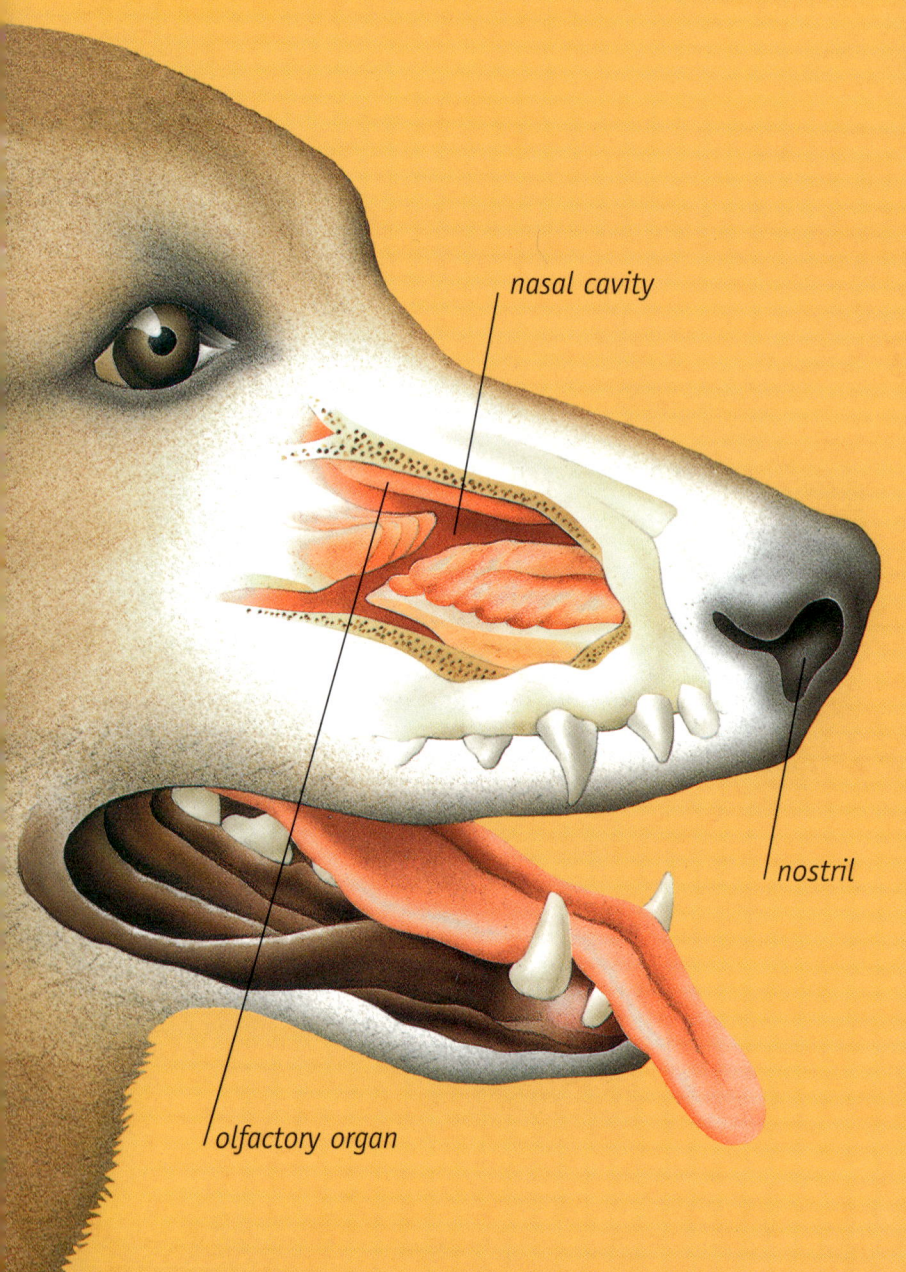

nasal cavity

nostril

olfactory organ

A mammal's nose

Inside a mammal's nose is a space called the nasal cavity. It contains a patch of hairs. This is the olfactory organ. When the animal breathes through its nose, air moves over the hairs. The nerves in the hairs send messages to the brain. These tell the animal about the smell.

A dog's sense of smell is 30 times stronger than ours. So dogs can pick up smells we could never pick up.

Smelly signals

Many mammals use smells to send each other messages. Deer rub strong-smelling juices on to trees. This tells other deer to keep away from their territory. Skunks are famous for their foul smell. They squirt a liquid from under their tails to scare off their predators.

A skunk squirting a liquid, which smells disgusting and stings the eyes of its predators.

Why can't I smell things when I have a cold?

When we have a cold our body makes extra mucus to protect it from the cold virus. The mucus fills up our nose so no air can get to the olfactory organ. This also makes it hard to taste things.

How do mammals hear?

Mammals get lots of information through their ears. They pick up messages about prey and predators and find out where they are.

Ear flaps

The part of the ear we can see is called the ear flap. Some mammals, like rabbits, have big ear flaps and this means they can hear very well. But seals have tiny holes on the sides of their heads, because big ears would slow them down when swimming. Many animals, like dogs and cats, can move their ears around so they can work out where sounds are coming from.

Inside the ear

Most of a mammal's ear is inside its head. The ear flap leads to a short tunnel. At the end of the tunnel is the eardrum. This tiny drum skin vibrates when sounds hit it, just like a drum vibrates when you hit it. The cochlea looks like a snail. It changes the vibrations from the drum into messages for the brain.

- ear flap
- skull bone
- nerve to brain
- cochlea
- semicircular canals
- eardrum
- ear canal

moth

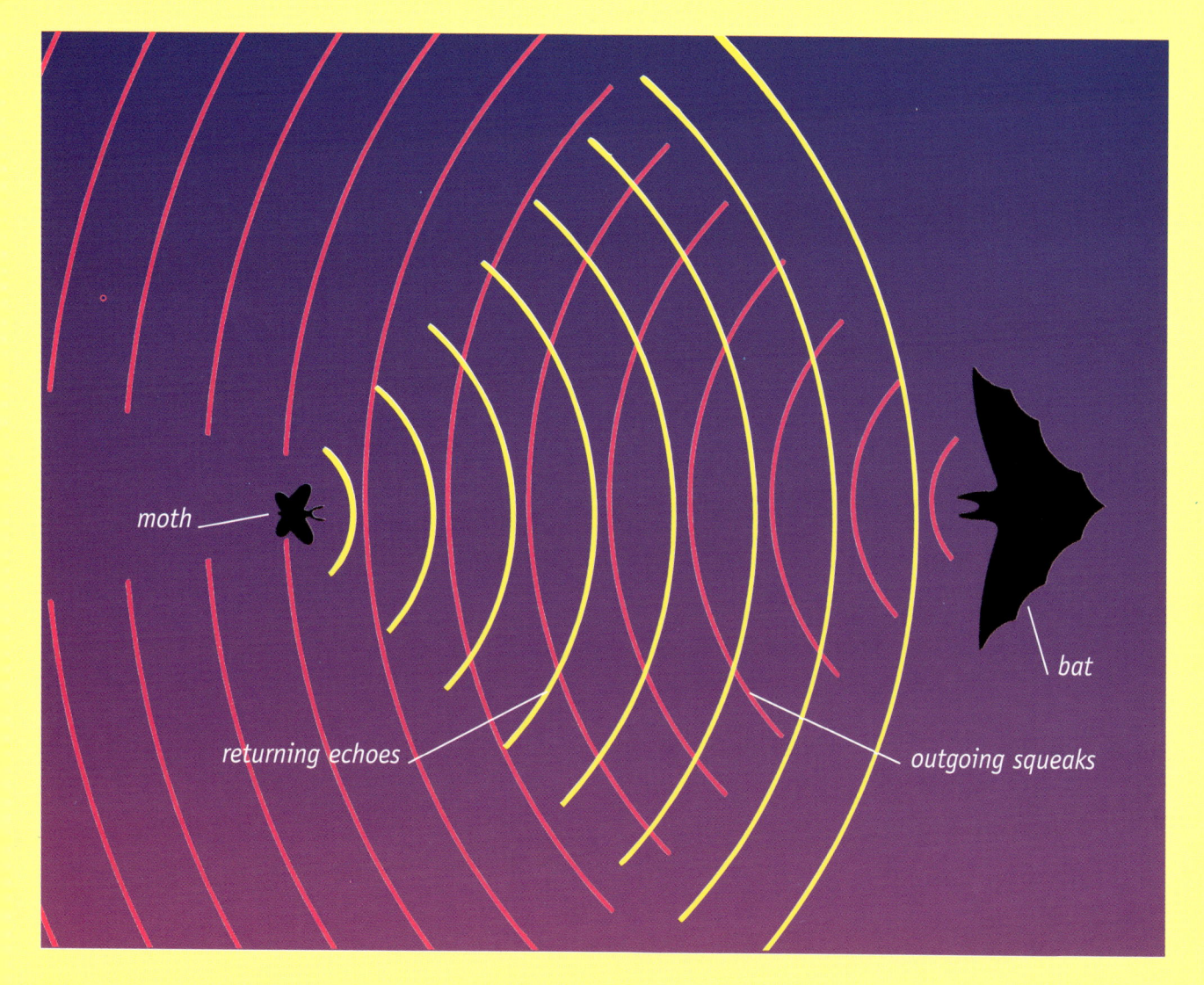

returning echoes

bat

outgoing squeaks

Bats use their amazing hearing to find out where they are and to find their prey. They send out tiny squeaks, then listen for the echo to work out where things are. This is called echo-location.

Why do I get dizzy when I spin around?

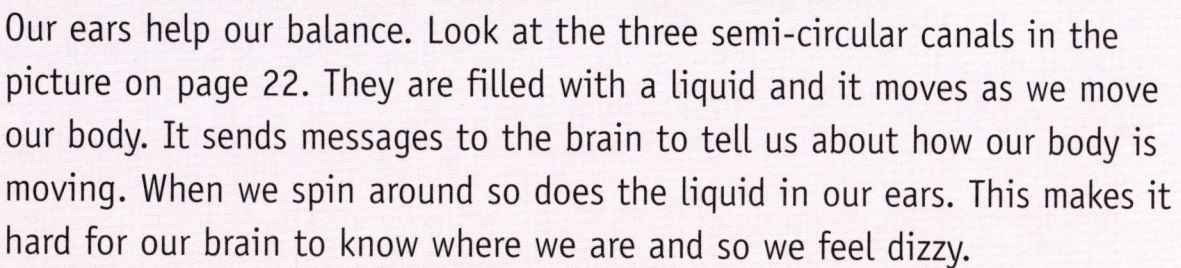

Our ears help our balance. Look at the three semi-circular canals in the picture on page 22. They are filled with a liquid and it moves as we move our body. It sends messages to the brain to tell us about how our body is moving. When we spin around so does the liquid in our ears. This makes it hard for our brain to know where we are and so we feel dizzy.

How do mammals see?

Mammals' eyes pass messages to the brain about shapes, colours and movement.

Inside the eye

A mammal's eyes can change to help it see in bright or dim light, close up or far away. The pupil is the black spot in the middle of the eye. It is a hole that gets smaller when the light is bright and bigger when the light is dim. The lens is just behind the pupil. It can change its shape so we can see things that are near or far away.

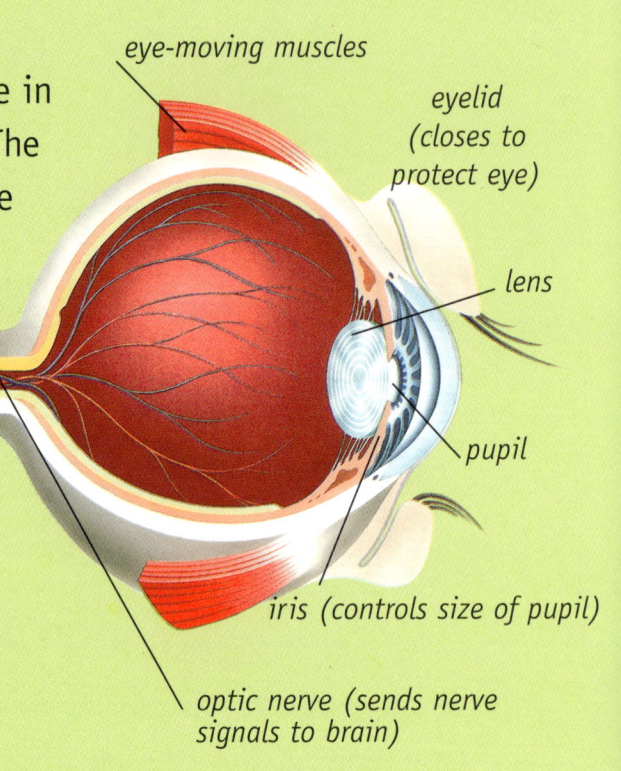

eye-moving muscles

eyelid (closes to protect eye)

lens

pupil

iris (controls size of pupil)

optic nerve (sends nerve signals to brain)

Eye sizes

Nocturnal animals, like bushbabies, have big eyes so they can take in a lot of light. Animals that live underground, like moles, have tiny eyes because there's not much to see.

The bushbaby uses its sharp sight and keen hearing to hunt at night.

Predators and prey

Mammals that are hunters have eyes at the front of their heads. This helps them to focus clearly on the prey in front of them. Animals that are the prey of other animals, such as deer and rabbits, have eyes on the sides of their head, so that they can see predators creeping up on them.

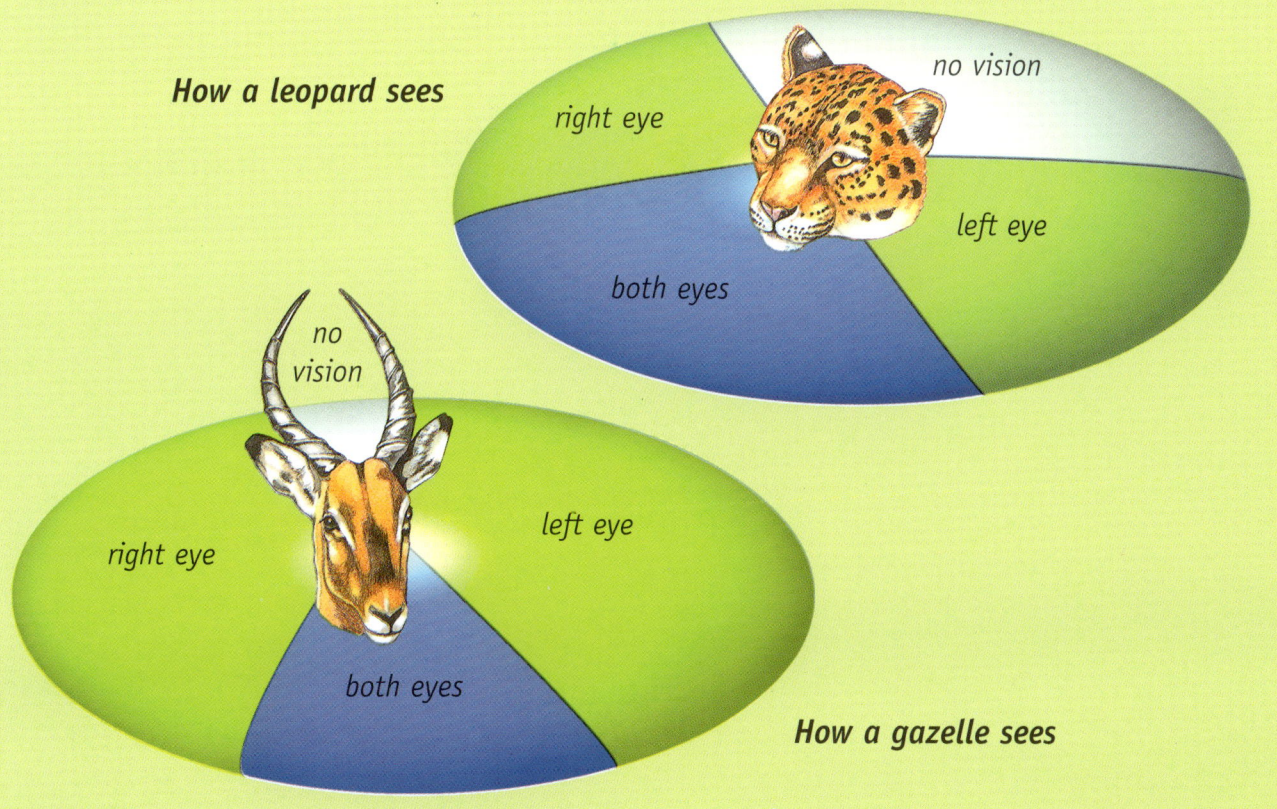

How a leopard sees

no vision
right eye
left eye
both eyes

no vision
right eye
left eye
both eyes

How a gazelle sees

Why do I blink?

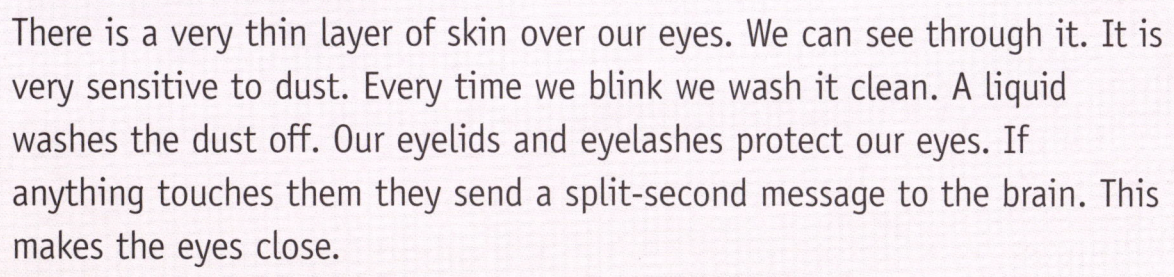

There is a very thin layer of skin over our eyes. We can see through it. It is very sensitive to dust. Every time we blink we wash it clean. A liquid washes the dust off. Our eyelids and eyelashes protect our eyes. If anything touches them they send a split-second message to the brain. This makes the eyes close.

How do mammals use camouflage?

Many mammals use camouflage to hide from predators. Some of the hunters use it to sneak up on their prey.

Changing coats

Some mammals change their coats at different times of year. In summer the Arctic hare has brown fur so it can hide in dry leaves. But in winter it grows thick white fur to hide against the snow.

This vole is very small. If it sees or hears danger, it does not move. It hopes that a predator might think it is a dead leaf and go away.

Spots, stripes and other patterns

Some mammals have patterns on their coats. In the woods at night, a badger's stripes look like moonlight coming through the trees. A zebra's stripes are useful when there are a lot of zebras together. They all mingle and it is very hard for a predator to pick out just one animal to hunt.

The ocelot's stripes and spots make it very hard to see it by moonlight.

When I cut my hair, why doesn't it hurt?

Our hair and nails are made up of dead cells. They haven't got any nerves so they can't send messages to the brain. But if someone pulls our hair we yell! We do have nerves where the hair comes out of the head. They are called hair roots and they send messages to the brain. That's why we feel pain.

How do mammals' babies grow?

Most baby mammals grow inside their mother's body. They grow in her womb and get their food and oxygen from her. After they are born, their food is their mother's milk. Most mammals look after their young until they can look after themselves.

Marsupials

Some mammals are a bit different. Marsupials only spend a short time in the mother's womb. A baby kangaroo is tiny when it is born. It has no fur and cannot see. It has to crawl into its mother's pouch or it would die. Inside the pouch it keeps warm, drinks its mother's milk and grows until it can look after itself.

A kangaroo with its young, or 'joey'

Monotremes

There are three mammals which lay eggs. They are called monotremes. When the eggs hatch, the young drink their mother's milk, just like all the other mammals.

This platypus is guarding its nest.

Why do babies and children like to play?

When children play they are practising skills they will need when they grow up. They are learning to move, to make themselves understood and to get on with people.

Lots of other mammals play too. They are also practising the skills they will need in later life. That's why puppies chase each other and kittens jump on balls. They are practising their hunting skills.

Answers

Answers to 'Name the skeleton' on pages 6 and 7

1. sea lion
2. pronghorn
3. kangaroo
4. bear

Glossary

contract
to shorten

evolve
to change gradually from one generation to the next

mucus
a slimy substance produced by the lining of the nose and throat

nutrient
a substance in food which helps animals and plants to grow and stay healthy

predator
an animal that kills and eats other animals

prey
an animal killed by another animal for food

suckle
to feed a young animal on its mother's milk

vibrate
to move backwards and forwards or up and down very quickly

virus
a germ that can cause disease

Index

Arctic hare 26
badger 27
bats 5, 11
   echolocation 23
bear 7, 12, 13, 30
blood 4, 16, 17
body temperature 4, 12, 14, 17
brain 18, 19
   brain stem 19
   cerebellum 19
   cerebrum 19
   hypothalamus 18
bushbaby 24
camel 13
cat 8, 24
chamois 14
cheetah 10, 11
deer 21, 25
digestive system 12, 13
   intestines 12, 13
   mouth 12
   stomach 12, 13
dog 20, 22
dolphin 10
elephant 13
energy 12, 14, 16
evolution 5
eyes 24, 25
gazelle 25
giraffe 6
hare 11
horse 5, 6, 11, 22

humans 5, 7, 9, 11, 13, 15, 17, 18, 20, 25, 27, 29
   blood 17
   breathing 15
   digestion 13
   eating 13
   hearing 23
   movement 7, 11
   muscles 9
   nerves 18, 27
   play 29
   seeing 25
   skeleton 7
   smell 20
kangaroo 7, 10, 28, 30
leopard 25
marsupial 28
mole 24
monkey 5
monotreme 29
muscles 8-11, 15, 18, 19, 24, 29, 31
   contraction 8, 9
   cramp 9
orang-utan 10
otter 10
pronghorn 7, 30
rabbit 22, 25
respiratory system 14,
   alveoli 15

   bronchiole 15
   coughing 15
   exercising 15
   lung 14-16
   nose 14
   throat 14, 15
   windpipe 14, 15
sea lion 6, 30
seal 5, 22
skeleton 6-8, 10
skunk 21
sloth 11
speed 11
tiger 9
vole 26
weightlifter 9
whale 4, 5, 10, 14
zebra 27